"In *Start Next Now*, Bob Pritchett provides an incredibly efficient way to discover specific, practical steps to advance yourself professionally, personally, and spiritually. He also explains one of my passions, which is the relationship between compensation, happiness, and meaningful work, and how to find the right balance."

DAN PRICE Founder and CEO, Gravity Payments

"In working with dozens of young leaders in my church and through my blog readership, the one thing they seem to want most is assurance from those of us who have gone before them. They want someone who believes in them and will give them permission to try. And, if they fail, to try again. This is a needed book for our culture and our times."

RON EDMONDSON Pastor and organizational leadership consultant, RonEdmondson.com

"It took me years to wrap my mind around how to reach my goals. The advice in *Start Next Now* has been immensely helpful and helps me not only pursue more purposefully my own goals, but also help others achieve theirs! A light read with heavy truth that will stand."

JAMES NWOBU Chief operating officer, Collision Records

"Anyone looking for the final (or first) push toward realizing the life they have always wanted should stop what they are doing and read Bob Pritchett's book. We all strive for our 'Next Now,' but oftentimes fail to break it down into the pragmatic steps required for forward progress. As he says in the book, 'Ambition is a treadmill,' and Bob will help change the way you think about things just enough so that you can get on the treadmill tomorrow."

TODD GARLAND founder and CEO, BuySellAds

"Bob Pritchett has outlined simple and highly effective strategies for taking your reality to the next level. Through compelling stories and practical advice, *Start Next Now* will help change your paradigm. It is blunt, real, and highly engaging—a must-read, chock-full of motivation to challenge your status quo and get you focused on reaching your goals. Bob's inspiring and in-your-face perspectives will become bullet points for leadership training experts for years to come. So, there is no time to lose. Stop reading this endorsement and start reading Start Next Now. You will be glad you did!"

JOHN BORNSCHEIN Vice chairman, National Day of Prayer Task Force

"Bob wants to help you be successful at work, but more importantly, he wants to help you uncover your passion in life. Do you long to live a life of purpose? Do you want to be effective and make a difference with your life? This book is teeming with practical advice you can implement into your life instantly. A quick, enjoyable, and very important read for young people, or people of any age for that matter."

MATT BROWN Evangelist, author of *Awakening*, and founder of Think Eternity

"It is a thrill to read *Start Next Now*. We find many excuses to not get started or follow through on our dreams, but Bob points out many steps and pitfalls. He shows us his thoughts to help us gain courage. Realize *now* that it is the courage that you earn in the journey that is the success. The book is an easy read and a pocket pal worthy of sharing."

BECKY RANEY Chief operating officer, Print & Copy Factory

"Bob is a true entrepreneur who has been there, and done that. *Start Next Now* is an honest look at what it takes to be successful in business and life with practical advice that you can implement today."

ANNE-MARIE FAIOLA Founder, Brambleberry.com and SoapQueen.com

"*Start Next Now* is a concise plan for those who find they have more to achieve and aren't sure how to do so. I would recommend this quick read to any person starting in a career or simply stuck at a level of employment below their true potential."

JANE CARTEN CEO, Saturna Capital

"Just entering your career and need guidance? Stuck in your job and need direction? Doing ok but not moving forward? *Start Next Now* is for you! Biblical, balanced, witty, clear, honest, practical advice for getting the life you've always wanted."

DR. MARK FUTATO Professor and author

"Whether you have a giant goal or a modest one, *Start Next Now* will get you moving in the right direction and guide you along the path of success. Bob Pritchett has been there and done that in dramatic but humble fashion, and he can help you achieve your goals as well."

MARK DONNELLY #1 *New York Times* bestselling author of multiple *Chicken Soup for the Soul* books

"*Start Next Now* is full of sage advice from someone who practices what he preaches. Every HR department should have this resource available for their employees."

MATT LUCAS Provost and executive vice president, Corban University

"I plan to have each of my six children read this book—but there is no one who cannot learn something from *Start Next Now*. This book gives each person an opportunity to fail at something and learn from it, so they can be ready for the next venture. When done with the attributes of Christ, we can certainly use our vocation to further the cause of Christ, not only in others' lives, but in our own."

DR. MARK CHAVALAS Professor and author

"Bob Pritchett has a knack for taking complicated concepts and presenting them in simple, memorable ways. He shares a wealth of practical wisdom on accomplishing life goals. This is a book I'm going to give to my children and to young entrepreneurs to help them chart a meaningful course for their lives."

BRIAN MACKAY Principal, Marketplace One

"*Start Next Now* gives you the courage to pursue goals...along with massively practical tips to help you get started today."

GABE COOPER Founder and CEO, Brushfire Interactive and Virtuous Software

"Bob Pritchett offers a lot of insightful, timeless advice that you'll find valuable for you, your kids, employees, managers, or anyone wanting to get ahead. I'd strongly urge you to read and share *Start Next Now*."

TONY LARSON President, Whatcom Business Alliance

"*Start Next Now* will breathe new life into your career, and set new purpose to your personal and business goals. It will help you consider the 'why' in your life and challenge you to succeed."

TROY MULJAT Commercial real estate developer

"I love this book, the perfect gift for friends and employees looking to get unstuck. I encounter so many friends who talk about making a change in their life but don't know how to start. This quick and easy read is a practical resource to jump-start their journey. Understanding Imposter Syndrome definitely shifts your mindset to take on huge challenges. I will definitely be getting every one of my employees a copy of this book to encourage them on their path."

TODD WATSON CEO, Showit, Inc.

"In a time when everyone desires authenticity but few display it, Bob Pritchett stands out. Bob is self-taught and self-made, and he accomplished both by practicing the principles he shares in this book. *Start Next Now* is Bob's generous (and blunt) offer to help you accomplish your goals. It may not contain everything you need to know in order to succeed, but you need to know everything in it to have a fighting chance."

JAMES J. KRAGENBRING CFA, president and chief investment officer, Aquifer Capital, LLC

START NEXT NOW

HOW TO GET

START

THE LIFE

NEXT

YOU'VE ALWAYS

NOW

WANTED

BOB PRITCHETT

KIRKDALEPRESS

Start Next Now: How to Get the Life You've Always Wanted

Copyright 2015 Bob Pritchett

Kirkdale Press, 1313 Commercial St., Bellingham, WA 98225
KirkdalePress.com

Print ISBN 978-1-57-799645-3
Digital ISBN 978-1-57-799646-0

Kirkdale Editorial Team: Lynnea Fraser, Abigail Stocker
Cover Design: Josh Warren
Typesetting: Brittany VanErem

Contents

INTRODUCTION:
PERMISSION TO TRY ANYTHING

My parents were not particularly ambitious for me.

They didn't push me to excel in school. My dad didn't pressure me to win the game, and my mom wasn't overly concerned with my report card. My parents cared a lot about my character but not as much, it seemed, about preparing me for a specific career or status or ambition. They didn't push me to do anything in particular.

What my parents did give me was encouragement to find and explore my own passions. Every project, idea, and fleeting career ambition was met with their encouragement, support, and a suggestion of what I could do *right now* to explore that passion.

When I expressed an interest in bees, they put a beehive in the backyard and encouraged me to start a honey business.

When I wanted to be an FBI agent, my parents introduced me to a police detective who gave me a stack of professional law enforcement magazines. When I expressed an interest in bees, they put a beehive in the backyard and encouraged me to start a honey business. My interest in business got me sent around the neighborhood with a cart selling vegetables from the garden; my curiosity about journalism was met with the support to launch a school newspaper.

I have read many stories about parents driving children toward excellence in one pursuit or another, but none of parents giving such benign and nonspecific support as I received. Athlete, merchant, cop, or president of the United States—my parents led me to believe that every option was open to me, and they offered suggestions on how to start exploring it *right now.*

My interest in computers led to a high school business selling software for computer programmers. In writing and online no one knew I was just a kid, and during the day my mother took phone messages so I could return calls after school.

That experience helped me land an internship at Microsoft when I was eighteen. A year later I was working full time at Microsoft when I started a hobby project with a friend that grew into yet another business. At twenty I left to pursue that business full time, and I am still leading it more than twenty years later.

I love being an entrepreneur; it's fun to set a vision and lead a team and even make some money. But the joy I find in my daily work doesn't come from money or position, but rather from doing purposeful work I love with people I love. And I am wise enough to know that I am not a self-made man. I am the beneficiary of many advantages, not the least of which is permission.

Today I employ hundreds of people. In interviews and coffee conversations, I hear over and over again how people were held back by parents who discouraged them, by teachers and

You have permission to do something incredible.

coaches and bosses and counselors who told them they weren't qualified, and by so-called friends who laughed at their dreams.

If you are among those who did not find encouragement to pursue your passion, then I am here to pass along the wisdom of my gently supportive parents: You have permission to try anything and my belief that you can accomplish whatever you'd like. It might be hard, it might take time, and maybe you won't even want to. But we can start finding out *right now*.

You have permission to do something incredible.

You can have the life you've always wanted.

You can start your next now.

STEP 1

IDENTIFY YOUR
NEXT

— WHAT DO YOU —
WANT?

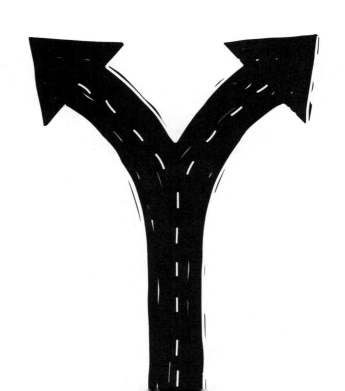

Before you can achieve the life you want, you need to figure out what that is.

Your goal may be about doing something. You may want to write a book, record an album, create a product, or launch a company.

Your goal may be about getting a position: You may want to be able to protect others, to teach, or to motivate.

Your next can reflect your desires or even your personality. You may find online tests for skills, attitudes, and personality to be useful in helping identify strengths you can build on or weaknesses you should watch out for.

Is there something that comes easily to you that others find difficult? Work with your strengths. It is easiest to distinguish yourself in the areas where you have unique experience or skills. Take a personal inventory of your strengths; what's the most unusual among them? What would happen if you invested more in developing and even showcasing this strength?

What things make you feel energized? What do you find yourself thinking about in your free time? Examine these and determine what exactly it is that you want to do to have the life you've always wanted. Envision what that will look like.

Maybe you don't have a goal and don't even feel a need for one. You can still move ahead by identifying a passion and choosing to pursue it at the next level: Record an album of your music, publish your writing, enter your photography in a contest, or get paid to do your hobby.

Figuring out what you want can actually be the most diffi-cult part of getting ahead. Don't worry—there isn't a perfect answer, and you can always change your answer. If you can't identify the big goal down the road, at least identify the next thing you want to try.

MONEY

DOESN'T BUY HAPPINESS

When people think about "getting ahead," they often assume it means "making more money."

More money seems like success, and fame and power are classic side dishes. Of course we all want happiness—that's a given. It sounds better too: It's easy to say we want "happiness" and know that it implies money too. Right?

I will tell you that studies have shown that money does buy happiness—up to around $75,000 per year. That's enough money to avoid many of the discomforts and inconveniences that come from not enough funds. But after that middle-class level, more money doesn't equate to more happiness.

I've made more money, and I have had the opportunity to spend time around people who have made *a lot more* money. While having money has its fun moments, I've come to believe that the Bible offers the best observation about money:

"When prosperity increases, those who consume it increase. So its owner gains nothing, except to see his wealth before it is spent." –Ecclesiastes 5:11 LEB

In other words, you can only eat so much steak and lobster. The rich may order a higher-grade steak, but they start picking up the check for an ever-growing table. (An entourage may be a sign that you're important, but it's also a lot more mouths to feed.) If you get a chance to bring in more than a middle-class income, you'll be amazed at how quickly you're buying steak and lobster for other people. There's nothing wrong with that, but if you want to hold on to happiness, you'll need to make sure it's generosity, not greed, that characterizes your feelings about money.

When most people think of wisdom on money, they misquote the Bible and say, "Money is the root of all evil." The Bible actually says, "The *love of money* is a root of all evil" (1 Timothy 6:10 LEB, emphasis mine). (The Bible also says a lot more on the subject; it's worth checking out.)

My success in business has given me a taste of money, fame, and power, and I know them to be strong temptations. But I've also found them to be hollow pleasures compared to doing something I believe is important alongside incredible people I love.

I hope you are pursuing something that will let you jump from bed each morning excited to start your day and then collapse into bed each night knowing you did something with purpose.

> **"Success is getting what you want.**
> **Happiness is wanting what you get."**
> **–Dale Carnegie**

"I don't belong here," a rising star in my company confided to me.

"I come from a blue-collar family, and I was going to work in the family restaurant. I'm not really qualified to be managing anybody."

So I felt like an idiot. I recognized this guy's talent, willingness to work hard, and ability to take advice and learn new things. I promoted him into leadership. And now he was telling me I picked the wrong guy.

Maybe I made this mistake because I don't really know what I'm doing in business. I didn't finish high school, dropped out of college, and had less than two years of experience in the workforce before starting this company, which has swung from huge success to near failure to stable business over the years.

A professional manager wouldn't have made this mistake, I chided myself. *Maybe I should have stayed in college and then gotten an MBA. Then I would know what I'm doing messing around with people's lives and careers.*

HOGWASH.

My employee was suffering an episode of Imposter Syndrome, and he was drawing me into it as well. You've probably experienced it too: the feeling that you are in over your head, that you don't know what you're doing, and that any moment your boss / teacher / peer will call you out on your incompetence and send you scurrying off the stage in shame.

It's true: You are in over your head. There are deserving people who would be better at your job. Whatever you want to do next, it won't be as good as you'd like, and someone may even point that out. You could be exposed.

The good news, though, is that you aren't alone. Almost everyone suffers episodes of Imposter Syndrome, and in the same way they are all imposters. The number one draft pick, America's top CEO, and the celebrity role model of the year all know there's a more deserving honoree, and your favorite band and novelist are right this moment wracked with fear that the next album or book will reveal they are out of ideas and their recent success was just a fluke.

If you're feeling like a fraud, don't worry: You're in good—and plentiful—company.

The only people who never suffer Imposter Syndrome are sociopaths and narcissists, and they certainly haven't kept reading this far. They don't need anybody's permission.

So if you're feeling like a fraud, or like someone who might not be able to do it, don't worry: You're in good—and plentiful—company.

So let's just accept that you and I are both undeserving of our current blessings and unqualified for greater success. That's all true. Now let's move on to achieving your next undeserved success with gratitude and humility.

STEP 2

START
DOING
THE NEXT THING
NOW

ALWAYS

TURN TO GOAL

Now that you know what you want, start moving in that direction.

It may not be possible to move directly to your goal, but you can make sure that every turn you make is in the direction of your goal. Imagine yourself moving down a sports field with the ball; there may be a defender on the straight line between you and the goal, and you may have to zig left or zag right. What you don't want to do is run in the opposite direction or give up territory. Keep moving, and keep turning toward the goal.

When people interview with me, I ask, "What do you want to be doing five years from now?" All too often I hear that their career ambition is something completely different than what they are interviewing for. Taking the job with my company doesn't move them toward their goal. It's a detour.

> **There may be a defender on the straight line between you and the goal, and you may have to zig left or zag right.**

You may not be able to jump right into your dream job. If so, look for a job in the same industry, or where you'll develop skills that will help you in your dream job. There is so much to learn in every field that you shouldn't be wasting time acquiring completely irrelevant skills. Use your time intentionally. You may need to take an entry-level job to pay the bills, and that's okay. But take an entry-level job that represents a turn toward your goal.

You can apply this logic to all the ways you use your time: Choose classes that will teach you things you need to know to achieve your goal. Volunteer where you will develop skills you'll need in the future.

Always turning toward your goal not only keeps your goal in mind, but it also helps you acquire the knowledge, the connections, and even the vocabulary that will help you achieve your goal.

Many people set their goal so far in the distance that they don't feel like they have to do anything today.

They are waiting.

Waiting for permission.

Waiting for a promotion.

Waiting for a recruiter to call.

Waiting for the timing to be right.

Waiting for someone to tell them what to do next.

Waiting for someone to notice they are waiting.

Waiting for someone else to do something.

Waiting for a change that is never going to happen on its own.

STOP WAITING.

The space between here and your goal is not filled with time. The space between here and your goal is filled with changes.

Very little happens on its own. If you are here and you want to be there, something needs to change.

Being picked up by aliens or a benevolent boss or the Nobel Prize Committee and magically transported from your present state to your future goal is a low-probability event. The only likely path from here to your goal is a large number of changes.

There are very few mandatory minimum time delays between changes. There are, in fact, few mandatory change steps. Everyone's path involves a different sequence of changes.

To arrive at your goal sooner, increase your rate of change.

The space between here and your goal is filled with changes.

A side effect of increasing your rate of change is that the price of each change goes down. A quick turn in the wrong direction is just as quickly corrected. When you are able to make changes quickly, you'll be less afraid of making the wrong change.

If you're going to get ahead in the world, you're going to have to get comfortable with being uncomfortable.

When you've mastered the skills for your goal, or when you're the go-to person for questions in your area, there's a certain feeling of security that's very comfortable. It's also a sign that you aren't growing or moving ahead.

IGNORANT. INCOMPETENT.

We treat these words as insults and cringe when they're directed our way. And if we feel in these insults the sting of truth, we want to escape—to hide somewhere safe and comfortable where our shame won't be called out.

Ignorant and incompetent aren't elements of our character; they are descriptive terms for a temporary state of affairs.

But ignorance and incompetence are nothing to be ashamed of. *Ignorant* and *incompetent* aren't elements of our character; they are descriptive terms for a temporary state of affairs. I was once ignorant of Shakespeare and algebra and the joys of being a parent. I was incompetent at computer programming and riding a bicycle and frying an egg. Today I know these things and have acquired these skills, even as I remain ignorant and incompetent in countless other areas.

Ironically, it's not the areas in which our ignorance and incompetence are the largest that we're most uncomfortable. I know nothing of Eastern European literature, and I'm fine with that. I have no skills in kiteboarding, and that doesn't bother me.

It is ignorance and incompetence in the next things—the adjacent areas where we'll find the knowledge and skills to help us take the next step—that make us most uncomfortable. As the leader of a growing business, I'm a bit embarrassed by my ignorance of statistics and business financial reports. I am uncomfortable that I don't have the public speaking skills required at the next level of engagements. It is tempting to stay in my comfort zone, to have others conduct the rigorous financial analysis of my business, and to limit my speaking to smaller audiences.

If you are comfortable, you aren't moving ahead.

The next thing you need to know or do is essential to taking the next step, and it's the thing that will make you the most uncomfortable. You need to embrace this discomfort. People who are learning and growing are by definition continually ignorant and incompetent. Claim your ignorance and incompetence, address them, and then seek out yet another level of ignorance and incompetence. This is the ladder of growth.

If you are comfortable, you aren't moving ahead.

Fear is the fence that bounds our success.

What was the safe zone of your childhood? The backyard? This side of the street? Up to the woods? Down to the corner?

Parents put an imaginary (and sometimes real) fence around children; stay inside the fence, and you're safe and can do what you want. But beyond the fence lies danger—from strangers, creeks, dogs, or cars—and you can't go there without permission or an escort.

We tend to live our lives in similar safety zones.

"I know how to do this job,
  but I don't know how to manage people."

"I can lead a meeting,
  but don't ask me to speak onstage."

"I take photographs for myself,
  but nothing good enough to hang on the wall."

"I can create the product,
  but I can't read the financial statement."

"I'll sing 'Happy Birthday' with the group,
  but don't give me a microphone."

Our safety zones are fenced in by fear. We fear we don't have permission. We fear we are ignorant. We fear we are incompetent. We fear we have too much to lose. We fear we can't afford the cost. We fear we might fail.

We've already dealt with permission: You have it.

We've addressed ignorance and incompetence: true, and surmountable.

But it's still possible that we have too much to lose, or can't afford the cost, or might fail.

The risk of moving your fence—of expanding your safety zone—might be too high. I'm not going to tell you never to be afraid, because fear can be beneficial.

Fear is what causes us to consider risks and to count costs, and that's a very good thing. Fear is what keeps us from climbing tall, unstable ladders. Fear is what keeps us from eating food prepared in unsanitary conditions. Fear isn't something we must eliminate, no matter what the pop-psychology T-shirts say. Fear can save your life.

> **I'm not going to tell you never to be afraid,** because fear can be beneficial.

Fear is, however, something you need to confront and evaluate. Fear is a useful feedback mechanism that can help us make wise decisions about risk, and getting ahead does involve risk. It may cost a lot to achieve your goal. The path forward may involve a lot of setbacks.

Don't risk what you can't afford to lose. It is worth taking some time to identify what you want to hold on to. Far too many people get so focused on their goal that they neither consider nor even realize the price they are paying to pursue it until it's too late. And often they lose what was dearest without even achieving their goal.

To achieve your goal would you:

... move to a new city?

... give up your marriage?

... work every weekend for a year?

... sell your grandfather's watch?

... sacrifice your relationship with your kids?

... embarrass yourself acquiring a new skill in public?

Your money, your time, your family, your dignity, your dog, your leisurely weekend brunches...decide what you can't afford to risk and watch those things carefully.

Do risk everything else. The annals of success are full of tales of sacrifice. And for every predictable sacrifice (time, money, or a marriage, for example) there are countless surprises: Steve Wozniak had to sell his calculator to help found Apple. Michael Bublé performed singing telegrams in pursuit of a singing career.

The annals of success are full of tales of sacrifice.

If you are going for your goal, if you are ready for what's next, you need to figure out what you aren't willing to risk, and then you need to be prepared to risk and possibly lose everything else.

Reaching your goal may not require everything, but it will certainly require something you did not expect.

Every decision is a risk. Inaction is just as much a decision as action, and it can be equally risky. It's usually less productive as well, since inaction is usually the "no-changes" decision, and achieving your goal depends on making changes.

Our big world is full of lots of people, and we all deal with this complexity by sorting people into bins.

At one level those bins might be nationality, race, level of education, or economic status. At another level they might be job title, floor-in-the-building, or gets-coffee-at-the-same-shop.

You are in a lot of bins, and an essential part of getting ahead is distinguishing yourself within the bins that matter for your goals.

There are a lot of traps here. The first trap is thinking that someone is carefully watching the bin and waiting to reward the best performers.

It is true that some organizations have processes for identifying good performers. School is designed to rank and sort and occasionally reward diligent students. The military and some large businesses have formal processes for reviewing and ranking staff. But these systems exist to meet the ongoing maintenance needs of the institutions, not to move you ahead as quickly as possible. "Serve your time, pay your dues, and we'll take care of you" is the shallow promise of a plodding organization. What it means is, "Sit quietly until we need someone, at which point we'll advance the person who best meets our needs."

This won't get you anywhere fast.

This won't get you anywhere fast.

A second trap is believing that there are standard ways to distinguish yourself, like formal education.

While it's true that education is the best investment you can make, diplomas and certificates aren't particularly useful in distinguishing yourself.

There are twenty thousand new high school valedictorians each year, and six times as many people earn an MBA annually. Harvard University has more than three hundred thousand living alumni. Sure, you can take your Harvard MBA to Lost Springs, Wyoming (population 4) and be the smartest person in town, but if you head to Wall Street to make your fortune, it will be hard to stand out among all your former classmates crowding the same elevators.

A diploma is a lot like the limited warranty on a refrigerator: an assurance that this unit meets a minimum standard of quality, just like each of the thousands of indistinguishable units the factory produced this year.

If you sit in a room full of people who have the same job title, or walk into an interview with a résumé certifying that your education is exactly the same as thousands of others, you might as well replace your name with a bar code, because you are just another unit from the factory.

Any common label (degree, certification, title, affiliation, etc.) marks you as a commodity. If everybody knows what it means to be a Stanford graduate or an accountant or an Eagle Scout or an NBA player, then it means enough people share that label—and the education and skills associated with it—that we can comfortably throw them together in a bin.

Titles are interesting in inverse proportion to the number of titleholders. And while you may have, or even want, a title shared by thousands, if you want to get ahead, you need to be distinguishable.

The way you distinguish yourself is by doing stuff. In particular, do distinct and useful activities that aren't easily labeled.

Do stuff that you couldn't represent by checking a box on a form. Do stuff your boss will have to explain (not apologize for!) when reporting to their boss. Do stuff that will be shared on the Internet. Do stuff that will cause interviewers to ask questions when they see it on your résumé.

> **Do stuff that will cause interviewers to ask questions when they see it on your résumé.**

This doesn't mean you can't check the boxes on a form; that may be necessary. You don't have to be radically creative and break all the rules. This isn't a call to deliver your weekly status report through interpretive dance.

Everything is relative. You don't need to be globally unique, with a one-word pop-star name and a unique personal brand. You just need to distinguish yourself from people with the same job title, people with the same education, people with the same goal as yours. If everyone is checking the boxes on the form, then you can too. But is there a note you should attach to that form? An extra step you could take? A way you could take ownership of a problem and find the solution?

INCREASE

YOUR

Familiarity bias advances people.

People prefer people they are familiar with. That familiarity doesn't have to be based on impressive and daring feats; it can be based on simple exposure. You, your name, and your work need to be visible to your peers, to your boss, to your boss's boss, to casual observers, to industry experts, to anyone who goes looking for you or your area of expertise on the Internet, etc.

Too many people toil away in obscurity, quietly working hard while they wait for a boss, a talent agent, or the fates to recognize their inherent worth and call them up for their reward.

It doesn't work that way. You've got to be seen.

I am not suggesting you become a shameless self-promoter, running toward cameras, volunteering for everything, slapping your name on documents, and annoying all your peers. But sitting quietly isn't going to move you toward your goal.

You have to own your exposure.

For every ten people with great press coverage, there might be one person who was pleasantly surprised that a journalist sought them out for a story. But the other nine worked really hard to earn that attention. (It is likely another few dozen worked hard at it, too, and still didn't manage to land the great press. Visibility takes work.)

It's the same in an office or school or within any organization: You have to own your exposure.

What is your name? Do people know your name? Sure, you pass lots of familiar faces in the hallways, and maybe you know who they are, but do they know who you are? Introduce yourself—repeatedly. If there's any chance that the coworker in the elevator, or an attendee at the meeting, doesn't know (or remember) your name, introduce yourself again. Many people have a hard time remembering names, particularly in large organizations. Even when people do remember names, they may forget if you're "Kir-sten" or "Keer-sten," or "Michael" or "Mike." No one wants to be embarrassed calling someone by the wrong name. Many would rather avoid you than admit their forgetfulness. Keep saying your name until they're saying it first.

Start Now: Name Badge Day

My company got large enough that I was forgetting names all the time. We created a Name Badge Day and got everyone "Hello, my name is…" tags to wear all day. Pop-up snack stations created reasons to gather and reintroduce ourselves.

You can create your own Name Badge Day in your organization—or just wear one yourself and see what happens.

Who are you? Someone may see you and think, *I remember your name, but I forgot what you do. I'll just look you up quickly on Google, LinkedIn, Facebook, or our organization's website.* Will that person find you by name? Will there be a photo so you aren't confused with someone else? Will it be easy to find the right Twitter account? @pancakefan4ever with a photo of syrupy goodness is a great way to express yourself anonymously, but it's not a great way to advance your goal. (Unless your goal is to rule the pancake industry.)

LinkedIn has become the de facto home of professional identity online. Make sure your profile is complete, with a photo and as much information as possible. LinkedIn is a way you can essentially post your résumé online without accidentally communicating "I'm looking for a new job!" to your existing employer. It's also the first place most people turn for information about you in a professional context. (And if you don't have a great LinkedIn profile people will keep looking, and they may find you in a less professional context such as Facebook or Instagram or somewhere else.)

Certain fields (law, graphic design, software development, etc.) have their own online communities for portfolios or occupation-specific content. Make sure your profiles are visible wherever people in your field will look, and try to use the same form of your name and the same photo whenever possible so people can associate the online information.

Start Now: LinkedIn

Go online and update your LinkedIn profile right now. Then send me an invitation to connect. Set up your profile on at least one other site.

What are you like? Help people become familiar with you. Don't be afraid to share personal interests, side projects, and even your ambitions in online profiles. At the least, it helps people who look you up see you as a more interesting and well-rounded person. It might even be the element of common interest that leads to an improved relationship or an offer of help.

Do stuff people see. Do you share a job title with a dozen people? It's possible you're known as "the one who sits fourth from the back on the left side." It would be far better to be known as "the one who wrote that proposal / drove the product to the upset customer / planned the party." It can be a big thing or a little thing; doing things increases your visibility.

Start Now: Clean Up

Don't know what to do to increase your visibility? If you share a workspace with others, there's one surefire way: Clean up. Chances are there's a mess near you right now. Clean it up. Organize the supply closet; clean the break room; straighten up the reception area; pick up litter in the parking lot. Nothing demonstrates ownership, responsibility, and attention to detail like cleaning when it's not your job. You may be able to subtly call attention to your work—"I put all the abandoned lunch containers in the upper-right cabinet"—but the best scenario is to be caught in the act of a pattern of helpful behavior.

Start conversations. People remember people they have a conversation with. Questions are a great excuse for a conversation, and people are flattered to be the source of answers. People like being flattered, and they will like you for showing them this attention, provided it's genuine and productive and not simply a manipulation.

Dress up. "Dress for the job you want, not the job you have." This is not a trite old saying that has lost its value in the age of the casual workplace; it is wisdom you can take to the bank. Dressing just as casually as all your coworkers is a signal that you're done moving up. It's a way to fit in and be invisible in the crowd. People who want to get ahead signal that to the people who can help them get ahead by dressing the part.

Are there billionaire entrepreneurs who dress in hoodie sweatshirts? Yes, and when you're a billionaire entrepreneur you can counter-signal too. But not until then.

Start Now: Dress Up

Dress up tomorrow. Just raise the bar one level beyond your norm, and be ready for comments from your peers. If you don't hear any, keep taking things up a level until you do.

Show up. You can't be seen if you aren't present. If 80 percent of life is showing up, as the saying goes, then 80 percent of people simply fail to do it enough. Be in the 20 percent. And when you keep showing up, opportunities will appear. Many people got their first job, their first break, or their first chance holding the microphone simply because they were familiar and available at a moment of need.

I am not suggesting that you need to be first in and last out at the office every day, that the boss should always find you at your desk on Saturday, or that you should volunteer for every event your charity puts on. Being visible doesn't mean stalking leaders or hiring a publicist. Being visible means not hiding, which is what so many people do unintentionally.

ASK QUESTIONS

You need to ask more questions.

Asking questions is one of the best ways to learn, grow, and achieve your goal. Most people know this instinctively at age three, when the world is full of wonder and all they want to know is "why?"

Rediscover your inner three-year-old.

Unfortunately, most people grow out of this insatiable curiosity on their way toward not growing anymore at all.

You would do well to rediscover your inner three-year-old, and today you'll still find receptive subjects for interrogation. Because while haggard parents quickly tire of being asked "why?" about the simplest things, adults who have acquired some expertise are flattered to be asked about it and eager to share what they know with thoughtful inquirers.

Asking questions is the heart of a great education, and learning how to ask questions will help you reach your goal more quickly.

Who to Ask

The short answer is: everybody. You can learn something useful from almost anyone, and often it's the unexpected source who delivers truly useful insight.

It's tempting to head to the top, seeking interviews with the celebrity or expert or CEO. And while these people may know a lot, they are usually polished interview subjects who have already shared their most interesting insights online or in published interviews. In an interview they are more likely to give practiced answers and inoffensive happy-talk than actionable insights.

Start asking questions right where you are. Talk to your peers, then people below or behind you.

Start Now: Make a List

Make a list of people you want to learn from.
Send an email to the first three people on the list
to schedule meetings.

What to Ask

The secret to asking great questions is remembering that everyone's favorite subject is themselves. When you are talking to someone who can help you learn more about reaching your goal, ask:

Why did you choose to do what you're doing?

What gets you most excited about your work?

What are the biggest frustrations you encounter
on a regular basis?

What do you wish your boss understood about you?

About your job?

What do you wish your subordinates understood about you? About your job?

What's the hardest thing about what you do?

If you were put in charge, what is the first change you'd make?

What is your short-term goal? What is your long-term goal?

How can I help you achieve your goals?

What question does no one ask you that they should?

Every question should be focused on the person you're asking.

Once you've surveyed the territory around and behind you, turn your focus to the people ahead of you, whether those who are higher up in your organization or who have done what you want to do somewhere else.

Every question should be focused on the person you're asking.

The same general questions and focus on your subject will be useful in these interviews, but you can also start being more direct in soliciting advice. If you're talking to someone you report to, be direct. You report to them, and it's appropriate to get (and follow) direct advice.

What do I need to do to get promoted?

What blind spot do I have that's holding me back?

How can I be more useful to you and the organization?

If you're talking to someone you don't report to, you can adopt language that puts the advice in more general terms, avoiding the awkward situation where you receive but choose not to follow specific personal advice. For example:

What advice would you give a young person who wanted to follow in your footsteps?

What do you wish you had done differently on the way to this position?

What do you wish you had known earlier in your career?

Interviewing the Powerful

Once you've mastered the art of asking good questions—and listening attentively and patiently to the answers—you can start approaching the powerful, such as celebrities, experts, and CEOs, who not only have succeeded in achieving goals like yours but who have the power to help advance you too.

The powerful are busy, but they can be surprisingly generous if you don't waste their time.

Do your research. Read everything you can about the person you plan to approach. Look for biographies, social media posts, published interviews, etc. Research will tell you who you know in common, what interests you might share, and the answers to lots of questions you were going to ask but now don't need to.

Have a good reason. Would it be cool to spend an hour asking questions of the president of the United States or the most recent winner of an Academy Award for Best Directing? Yes—and you could then spend years name-dropping at dinner parties. But unless you're a member of Congress or an award-winning indie filmmaker, it's likely that every answer you could extract from these famous people is already published in an interview somewhere. Don't waste their time or yours; seek to interview powerful people whose power is relevant to achieving your next goal.

Ask politely. Send an email with a small ask. Mention a common acquaintance or connection (school, previous employer, hometown, etc.). If possible, have a mutual acquaintance introduce you and ask on your behalf. Be as brief as possible, with the ask first and the background after.

Tell the person what you're going to ask. By including your questions in the introductory email, you communicate that you've done your research, that you aren't just trying to sneak in a sales pitch, and that you won't be wasting their time.

Here's an example email requesting a meeting.

TO: MRS.SMITH@LEADINGFLORIST.COM

FROM: YOUNGFLORIST@EMAIL.COM

SUBJECT: MEETING REQUEST

Mrs. Smith,

John Doe told me that you are the leading expert on what's happening in retail floristry.

I am just starting my career in floristry. I work in a small flower shop and have a passion for brightening lives with flowers.

May I have twenty minutes of your time?

I have nothing to sell you; I would simply appreciate learning from you. I'd like to ask:

How do you think the industry can respond to consumer enthusiasm for local products when the most popular flowers don't grow in every climate?

How do you identify great talent in floral design?

What was the most useful thing you read recently?

I can be available at your convenience.

Thank you for your consideration,

Young Florist
Email / Phone

SEND ✓

Once you get some time with a powerful person, make sure you use it wisely.

Don't ask the obvious questions. Nothing wastes time during an interview like asking a question you could have answered with a Google search. You should also avoid common questions like "What is your vision for your organization in the next five years?" When you've done your research before a meeting, you'll be able to ask specific, relevant questions.

Don't ask someone to mentor you. Mentorship is more often something that evolves out of a relationship than a job someone signs up for. While powerful people often enjoy being mentors and appreciate the chance to invest in someone younger, they are also wary of new obligations and formal commitments. If you have multiple interviews and are able to develop a correspondence, you may find yourself being mentored without calling it that. It's even okay to ask at some point, but only when you have built up a relationship and rapport.

Don't ask for much. There is a school of thought that every meeting is a waste if you don't make an ask. I am inclined to think of the answers to your questions as being a great and valuable takeaway. If you have an audience with a powerful person who can help you achieve your goal, the most important thing you can leave with is a relationship. When you make too big an ask, you risk turning a pleasant and flattering opportunity to share wisdom with an up-and-comer into *yet another uncomfortable meeting where I had to say no to someone.*

One way to soften your requests is to phrase them as ignorable options. While this is a terrible technique in sales, it can be a useful technique in building relationships with people ahead of you.

"I would really enjoy spending a summer as an intern at your company."

"If you'd be comfortable making an introduction, I would really appreciate it."

Follow up. After your interview, follow up with a simple thank-you note. (This can be an email nowadays, though a paper thank-you note may be more appropriate in some circumstances and will be more distinctive.) Be specific—"I really appreciated your insight about…"—and make sure your gratitude is not phrased in a way that requires a response or puts any further obligation on the recipient. If possible, include some kind of gift: a link to an article relevant to your conversation, an open-ended offer of an introduction to someone you know, etc.

Someone knows the answer to every question you have about advancing your career, launching a project, or making more money. Even more importantly, they have the answers to questions you don't have but should be asking.

Ask.

STEP 4

☑ EVALUATE

☑ YOUR

☑ EMPLOYMENT

Joining an organization is like getting on a bus.

You're part of a group, you're going somewhere together, and you may be able to travel further and at lower cost than traveling on your own. But you're not steering.

Make sure you are getting on a bus that will get you closer to your goal. There's no bigger waste of time than riding a bus that is going in the wrong direction.

Choose the Right Bus

Choosing where you work (or go to school) is an important decision. The need to generate income can create a lot of pressure to take the first job offer you get. But a thoughtful plan can help you land a better job, where you'll learn more, contribute more, be better rewarded, and move more quickly toward your goal.

To find the right job, your first and best tool is research. Whether you are looking for a new career or a job change, research your field and identify the companies that can best advance you along the path to your goal. Research people who do the job you're interested in doing. Look for opportunities to meet or correspond with people who work at the company. Check your social network for people who might be able to introduce you to people within the company. (There is a lot of truth in the old saying, "It's not what you know, it's who you know." And the only thing better than a warm introduction from outside the company is a warm introduction from inside the company.)

Once you have landed an interview you need to do even more research. Find out who you'll be meeting and research them online. Look for possible connections or shared experiences. Make sure you're current on news about the company, and read the corporate profile, history, and recent press releases. Ideally you should go into each interview knowing who you're going to meet, why they are trying to fill this position, and what their biggest challenge is right now.

I have conducted a thousand interviews, and I can let you in on a secret: The person interviewing you desperately wants to hire you. Companies don't hire people to stand around; they hire people because they need to get things done.

Interviewing dozens of candidates for a position is tedious, time-consuming, and an obstacle to getting things done.

Companies don't hire people to stand around; they hire people because they need to get things done.

Every interviewer goes into the interview hoping to find the perfect candidate, who is obviously right for the job and who will end the process and let them get back to work—now, with more help!

Every interview that doesn't result in a hire is a waste of two people's time. You can reduce this waste through research; your preparation will help you know if the position is a good fit for you (and let you avoid a pointless interview if it's not), and it will communicate all the right things to the interviewer:

that you're thoughtful, prepared, know what to do, and are willing to do it.

It may sound like a lot of work to research every job opportunity so thoroughly. But if thorough research is part of your process from the start, you won't need to prepare for dozens of interviews: A well-targeted approach to a best-fit job opportunity should land you a position quickly.

Get Off the Wrong Bus

If you are already employed, you should constantly be evaluating your experience and making sure it is still a good use of your time. You only have so much time in your life, and you will spend a large part of it at work. Are you investing that time at a place that will advance you toward your goal? Ask yourself:

Is there an opportunity to advance here?

Do I feel safe asking for feedback on my performance?

Is it safe to make a mistake in this organization?

Does my supervisor want me to succeed?

If I share my goal with people above me in the organization, will they help me achieve it, or see me as discontent or even a threat to their position?

If the answer to these questions is no, start looking for your next bus now.

Jobs Aren't the Only Buses

Sometimes a job isn't the best path toward the life you want. Volunteering for a nonprofit, creating a product, or joining a club might be the key to the education, connections, and opportunities you need to advance. Keep an eye out for buses going your direction, whether they look like jobs or not.

Your goal may be to be artistic, or to make a contribution, or simply to have a job that is a joy to head to each morning.

Whatever your goal, you will need to make money somehow. It helps to understand how money works, why you're only getting the money you are, and what you can do—if you choose—to make more.

Understand Who Is Responsible for Your Pay

Let's start with who is responsible for your pay:

You—not your mom, boss, professor, or the president of the United States—are the only person responsible for determining how much money you make.

You are the only person responsible for determining how much money you make.

We work in a market economy, and in a market economy the wages are set by supply and demand. While the market certainly prices all labor, you're the only individual who can directly influence your income by choosing what you do and how you do it.

In economic terms, you have monopoly control over the supply of your labor. Your labor can be something in high demand and short supply, in which case your monopoly power will allow you to charge a high price for your labor, or your labor can be something in low demand and high supply, in which case your monopoly power over a small unit of a commodity product will give you very little pricing power.

Understand Supply and Demand

You need to own the responsibility for the price of your labor and get a good understanding of the forces of supply and demand at play in your market.

What a job pays is not a statement about the inherent value of the people performing the job or the goodness of the employer or the priorities of a society. What a job pays is a piece of information about the supply of people who can do the job and the demand for that job to be done. For example:

Air Traffic Controller: $108,000 / year. This is a job that pays more than double the average salary. It's stressful, difficult, and requires specialized skills and personality characteristics. Not everyone has the training or can handle the complexity. The supply of people who can do the job is low.

Hand Laborers and Material Mover: $22,000 / year. Almost anyone can do hand labor and move stuff; no specialized education or skills are required. Many people are willing to do it to get a paycheck. The supply of people who can do the job is high, and consequently it pays half the average wage.

Hazardous Materials Removal: $37,000 / year. You don't need a lot more skills or education to get into this job, and what training is needed is available on the job. But fewer people want to move hazardous materials than nonhazardous materials, and so it pays significantly more.

Fine Art Landscape Painter: $0 / year. It's difficult to become a great fine art landscape painter. It can take years of study and practice to develop your eye, your technique, and the fine motor skills. Few people are qualified, and few people enter the field. The supply is very limited. However the demand is extremely limited too; who's hiring fine art landscape painters? The aristocracy isn't what it used to be, and so the wages for a full-time position in this field are approximately zero.

Teacher: not-enough / year. You don't have to wait long in America to hear a politician or activist wringing their hands over teacher salaries. "What does it say about our society that teachers are paid less than [some low status job]?" ask lots of people on TV. It says that our society has a near-endless supply of young people who would like to be teachers and who are willing to teach for low pay. Maybe they like inspiring kids, maybe they like being in charge of a room, or maybe they just loved being in school. The reason doesn't matter; the supply of potential teachers is enormous, and the demand is relatively fixed by population and demographics.

This is not a value judgment about teaching versus trash collection or sewage plant maintenance or custodial work. It's a reflection of supply and demand in the labor market. (Though I'd put the value to society of the latter positions right up there with teaching: Education leads to a better life, and good public health lets you live to enjoy it.)

This is not a value judgment. It's a reflection of supply and demand in the labor market.

You control how much money you make doing your job, and the most powerful tool you have is the choice of the labor market in which you introduce your supply. Is the labor you offer in low supply? Is it in high demand?

If you are going to introduce your labor into a market with high supply (teaching, for example), do everything you can to change your labor into something in low supply. The job title isn't the fullest description of the labor you supply; your attitude, initiative, ownership, and productivity are all parts of what you're offering. Can you take your commodity labor product and redefine it as something in low supply but high demand?

Maybe lots of people will do this job, but few will do it at night, or on call, or with enthusiasm. Find out what's in demand, what's in short supply, and tune your offering in the market. Then you can demand a higher price for your labor.

MONEY
IS ONLY PART OF THE PAY

Money isn't the only component of your compensation.

It's easy to get hung up on the numbers, and the numbers are easy to compare. But there are a lot of other benefits that make up your compensation.

Location

You're going to spend a lot of time at work. Is the location a benefit or a burden? Will you need to spend your vacation time compensating for your work environment and catching up on sunshine? Will a day at work give you energy or drain the life from you? What's it worth to have a five-minute commute versus hours in traffic?

Safety

How much pay is worth getting hurt? Some jobs are more dangerous than others, and these usually pay to reflect that difference. But are you being paid only slightly more for the extra risk, or are you being insured against long-term injury? An extra few dollars per hour doesn't help if you're no longer able to work. Sitting indoors in a chair all day is

How much pay is worth getting hurt?

dangerous to your health too. What's it worth being strapped to a desk versus being able to move around, changing locations and positions and settings?

Job Security

Depending on your circumstances, job security might be an important part of your compensation. This is part of the logic of a union, government, or academic job: the knowledge that you won't be suddenly unemployed. (Of course, if you're aggressively trying to move ahead, job security may be a low-value form of compensation.)

Autonomy

Would you rather be an independent agent or cog in the machine? There are lots of jobs where you're basically a humanoid robot in a fully controlled environment. Do you value acting independently, being trusted to consider information and make wise decisions, and to act autonomously? Do you value flexible schedules and control of your time? Autonomy is especially valuable when you're pursuing a goal and getting ahead.

Some people value jobs where there are no decisions to be made and where everything you need to know and do is fully explained in advance and where you can do the work on autopilot. But that's not a formula for getting ahead.

Purpose

Every job has a purpose. Your work will be more rewarding if you understand its purpose and if you're aligned with it.

You can spin almost any job as having a good or bad purpose. Try putting a job in the best and the worst light in order to see which description feels most accurate to you, and how it makes you feel. For example:

Fast-Food Worker

Good: A convenient meal for people in a hurry, an aid to harried parents, and a fun treat for kids.

Bad: Supporting a culture of shallow consumerism while pushing an obese public into an expensive public health crisis.

Attorney

Good: Advocate for the powerless, defender of rights and property, shepherd through a confusing and dangerous legal system.

Bad: A tax on productivity, a generator of paperwork and obfuscation, a defender of criminals, a parasite who feeds on the work of actual producers.

Blackjack Dealer

Good: Playing host to fun and affordable entertainment for people who have earned some relaxation.

Bad: Fleecing people who can least afford it by cynically manipulating their emotional reward system.

Car Salesperson

Good: Helping people find safe, affordable transportation that supports their work and play.

Bad: Talking people into spending beyond their means to feed their egos.

Tech Entrepreneur

Good: Finding innovative ways to provide services faster and cheaper using technology.

Bad: Destroying long-established industries and thousands of jobs while consolidating an entire industry's profits into the hands of one company's investors.

Which narrative rings true about the particular job you are considering? Which positive description would make you excited to do this job?

Community

You may spend more time with the people you work with than your family and friends. What is it worth to spend that time with people you like? With people who will help you move? Who will give you a ride to the airport? Who will listen to your relationship troubles? Who will bail you out of jail? You don't just take a job; you join a community.

You don't just take a job; you join a community.

I once met a man who had left a field that paid well to sell ice cream at Walt Disney World. He took a cut in pay, but every day he went to work and handed ice cream to kids. He got paid to show up every day at a place other people paid hundreds of dollars to enter. Was it worth it? To him it was, at that time. You need to decide what these other forms of compensation are worth to you.

GETTING A
RAISE

So you've got a job already; how do you get a raise?

First, face the fact:

The default annual raise for any position is zero.

You are engaged in a simple two-party relationship. You provide your labor to do this job, and the employer pays the agreed-upon wage to have the job done. Chances are, not much has changed since you entered into this agreement, and your employer isn't motivated to pay more now than before.

Sure, you may be offered a standard annual increase—a "cost of living" raise—but this is little more than a token payment to save the trouble and expense of filling your position if you leave. In fact, this cost of living increase is often explicitly tied to inflation, which is a mechanism for reducing wages over time. (Wages need to go up and down like all other costs in a market economy, reflecting changes in supply and demand. But there is a strong emotional aversion to reducing nominal wages—the numerical amount of your compensation. So inflation does the work of reducing everyone's income a little bit every year. A cost of living raise simply keeps your wages even; if you're getting less than inflation, you may be seeing an effective reduction in pay.)

Employers want to make more money, too, and one way they do that is by reducing, not increasing, the cost of labor. If you want to make a case for increasing the cost to your employer of your labor, you need to be increasing the value you are contributing—because ultimately everyone is paid for the value they add.

And in our generally free markets, you are always in competition with everyone in the world who can add the same value for the same, or less, cost.

It's tempting to believe that if you just keep doing your job you'll keep seeing increases in pay. And this can be true for a while: The cost of living raises add up over time. You become marginally more valuable to your employer as you acquire more skill and experience at your job. Some bosses just keep giving small raises in order to defer an awkward conversation.

Time in a seat adds very little value to most jobs.

But in the big picture, you won't see a significant increase in compensation if you don't make a significant change in your value contribution. Time in a seat adds very little value to most jobs.

The Danger of Continual Raises

Have you ever seen someone get let go from a mid- to high-level position after decades with a company and then struggle for months or even years before settling for a new job at dramatically lower pay? It's a tragic and oft-repeated scenario in large organizations.

Someone settles into a job and does it well. They ask for, or simply receive as a matter of course, incremental raises. Every year their cost to the organization is ratcheted up while their contribution remains the same. Their supervisors find it easier each year to give a raise and keep the experienced staffer in place than to endure the hassle of an empty position and a time-consuming search for cheaper talent.

So up and up the employee moves as the percentage increases compound, until one day something snaps: The job changes, the business is sold, cost-cutting measures are put in place, or the number simply becomes indefensible to the supervisor's supervisors. And suddenly the employee is on the street, unemployed and unemployable at their previous wage, which had long-ago lost its connection to their value contribution. (Or, in a common variation, it *was* connected to their value contribution, but a large part of their value was their knowledge of this particular organization, which is not transferable or valuable to another organization.)

One of the best ways to prevent this from happening to you is to be continually proactive in increasing your value, advancing your goals, and driving your own career. You should also make a point of maintaining skills and expertise that are valuable beyond one organization,

Start squirreling away resources for the rainy day. It's coming.

even if it requires switching organizations. And if you're in a position where you're comfortable and happy but where your job function might end, or where others might plausibly be hired to do it for significantly lower cost, start squirreling away resources for the rainy day. It's coming.

As a general rule, organizations don't like indispensable team members. When you are indispensable you have effectively taken the organization hostage, and while you may be able to collect a ransom (in the form of premium compensation) for some time, be assured that the organization is preparing to eject you in order to stop paying that premium.

CAN YOU AFFORD

THIS JOB?

There is a pay range for every job, and it's important to understand what the range is for your job.

Know the Pay Range for Your Job

The pay range is usually closely tied to the market wage for the labor being supplied, but within a specific organization there can be other factors that affect the top of the range.

The age of the organization. Unless they are exceptionally well funded, younger organizations usually pay less. Even if they have to pay market wages for a job function, they may only have the capacity (or willingness) to pay someone with entry-level skills in that job. They haven't been around long enough to have anyone with ten years of experience at that organization yet, and they won't pay for ten years' experience somewhere else.

The profitability of the company. If the company isn't making much money, it simply may not have the ability to pay more, no matter how valuable someone is.

The boss's salary. It's unusual for someone to get paid more than their boss. If there's a particularly frugal leader at the top of your organization, or if your manager would do their job for free and doesn't particularly care or need to make more, there's probably an artificial limit on your compensation. (Sales positions are the exception; it's not at all unusual for a top commission-based sales person to make more than their supervisor.)

It's one thing to know that the industry-standard wage for your job ranges from x to y, but it's more important to know what your organization's wage range is. You may have topped out already, in which case the chance you'll be getting a significant raise is very slim. You will have become like my perfect receptionists.

I have employed a number of perfect receptionists over the years. Receptionists start with an entry-level hourly wage. The job isn't complicated, but it can be hectic, and it takes a little time to learn the people, process, and organization. But over time most receptionists learn everyone's names, learn more about the organization and how to handle unusual requests, get skilled at handling more calls per hour, and so forth. And then they have become, for all intents and purposes, perfect receptionists.

Once you are the perfect receptionist, there's not much you can do to improve.

And that's when I've had to have the "this is the last raise you'll be receiving" conversation. Because once you are the perfect receptionist, there's not much you can do to improve. You can't be any nicer, you can't greet any more people, you can't handle any more calls, and there aren't any more skills to acquire for the job. Once you have mastered the job, the limits are physical: calls received, people greeted, minutes in an hour. You can be worth the top of the pay range, but it would be irresponsible of the organization to pay much more when so many people could do the job just as well for similar or less pay.

Upon hearing that there are no more raises to be earned, some receptionists are a little disappointed but happy to continue in the job. Some were planning to leave soon anyway to go back to school, and some just like the job and are happy to do it for the wage they are receiving.

Others want to know what they can do to earn more, and the answer is always the same: Move into a different job. And some do; one receptionist moved through several other positions in the company and eventually became a team lead in a technical position, earning significantly more than we ever paid a receptionist.

It is essential that you learn the pay range for your position and that you use that information to ask yourself: Would I be happy doing this job for the top of the pay range?

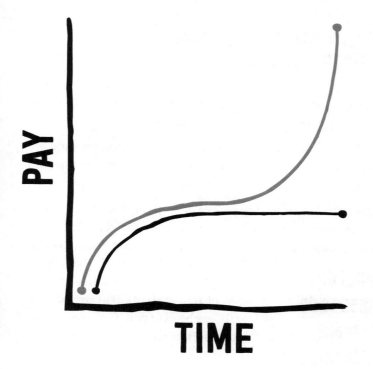

WOULD I BE HAPPY DOING THIS JOB
FOR THE TOP
OF THE PAY RANGE?

"Yes, I'd be happy doing this job for the top of the pay range."

Great news! You can stay where you are, at least for now. You just need to find out what's required to get from where your pay is now to the top of the range.

First, do your research. Read up on the job and the industry, and collect all the information you can on how the top-paid people in this job are different from you.

Next, start interviewing people. Talk to high performers and the people who are making the top of the range. Talk to your boss. Get all the information you can. Be honest with yourself about your strengths and weaknesses, and your level of skill at your job in comparison to those ahead of you. Once you've collected all this data and built your own best guess of what it will take for you to earn the top pay in the job you're in, go to the person who can pay you more and ask the question: "What do I need to do to make more money?"

What do I need to do to make more money?

Pay careful attention to the answer.

If you're in a growing organization that is constantly creating new opportunities, you're likely to get specific advice on exactly what to do. And this advice will be more useful than anything in this book or any other, because it's what the person presently negotiating your compensation wants you to know. You should treat this advice as the real answer and decide if you're willing and able to follow it.

If the answer is, "You just need to wait," then it's time to change jobs. Find another organization in which to do the same job, or look for a different job within this or another organization. Because "just wait" is just a way of holding down payroll costs.

There can be a legitimate reason for holding down payroll. Some organizations aren't growing. You might become twice as productive at your job, but the organization might be unable to translate that productivity gain into more revenue. For example, if I have an eight-seat restaurant, and people spend an hour at every meal staring at their smartphone no matter how fast you serve the food, a productivity gain in food prep or delivery isn't going to translate into more table turns or higher revenue. You can double your productivity without making a case for doubling your wage.

Lots of businesses don't see much growth (and many more are just shrinking very slowly). Their budget may not have the room for any growth. They may need to just repeatedly fill the same entry-level positions over and over again.

If this is the case, there's no need to be offended or upset; it's not about you. But if you want to get ahead, it is time to move on.

If nothing but time will advance your compensation, then there isn't much opportunity to grow and you need to move on.

It doesn't matter if you like the job and are happy with your current compensation. If there isn't a way you can get ahead, then you're wasting your time.

Note that "you need more experience" is a different answer than "you just need to wait." They sound similar and are often conflated, but they are different things. It's perfectly legitimate for an employer to pay more for more experience, and it is true that accumulating experience takes time. But experience and time don't advance in perfect synchronicity. You can waste a lot of time gaining no experience, and you can accelerate the acquisition of years of experience into less time.

There are two tools for acquiring experience faster. The first is simply doing more stuff. Is your job sales? Then sell more. If you can't sell more at your job, then sell other stuff on your own time. Have a garage sale; sell the junk in your basement at a flea market. Is your job writing press releases? If you can't write more than are needed each day at work, then volunteer for a nonprofit and write press releases on its behalf. Don't wait for experience to happen, just go and get it.

Don't wait for experience to happen, just go and get it.

The second tool for acquiring experience faster is reading. Other people have experienced a lot more than you, and the story of their experience and the insights acquired from it are written down as history and biography. You cannot read enough history and biography, and you'll find that books are available about the narrowest of fields as well as the most general of skills.

Start Now: Read Tonight

Start reading a relevant history or biography book tonight. Choose something about your industry, job function, or the skills you need to advance toward your goal.

"No, I wouldn't be happy making the top of this pay range."

If you wouldn't be happy with the top salary for your position, then it's time to find a new job. It's possible you simply need to switch organizations and do the same job function in another organization where there's a higher limit to the pay range. But it's also possible that you need to consider doing a different job function.

It can be difficult to change jobs in order to earn the income you'd like, and it can be emotionally challenging even to consider. You should give this a lot of thought and consider the costs of making a change, particularly if it's out of one field and into another.

Some job functions have a limited pay range, like the earlier example of teaching. Teaching usually doesn't pay a lot, but some people really enjoy it and would rather teach than do anything else. Don't let money cloud your thinking; be honest about what's most important to you.

There are people who do exactly what they want and who spend their time expressing their true selves without answering to anyone else. We call these people "artists." (Or, more commonly, "starving artists.")

But artists rarely make the top of anyone's desired pay range. Making more money always involves some kind of sacrifice. And the biggest element of that sacrifice involves what we do with the majority of our working hours: our primary job.

In our market economy, it is the jobs that others don't, can't, or won't do that pay more. Making more money may involve skills you haven't yet acquired or possibly can't acquire; it involves work you don't do now—and may not want to do. And the less you enjoy doing something, the more likely you'll be doing it poorly. You need to make these choices with your head and your heart.

You need to make these choices with your head and your heart.

I live with these choices too. I enjoyed my intense involvement in college journalism but chose not to pursue journalism as a career because I didn't want to be limited by the pay range. I spent years doing software development as my primary job function. I enjoyed it immensely and was able to steadily increase my pay as my skills improved. As a founder in a technology startup I could have chosen to stay with the technology job I loved and hired experienced businesspeople to provide executive leadership. But I realized that I was approaching the top of the pay range for a software developer, so I put it aside and focused on becoming an executive leader, where the pay range was bigger, with room to earn more.

Today I am happy with my compensation and comfortable with the top of the range available to the CEO of a company this size. I might be able to parlay my decades of business leadership experience into an even more highly paying position in a company with a larger market, faster growth, and brighter prospects, but I like the job I have and am content to have topped out on compensation. I am also choosing to stay in a position where I can see the path of continual growth I need to pursue to hold on to my job and where I anticipate continuing to enjoy that path.

The Peter Principle

In all this discussion of getting ahead and moving up, we are assuming that you are up to the task.

And I believe that to be true. With the right attitude—which you are exhibiting simply by reading this book—you can accomplish anything, and history has proven that persistence can eventually overcome almost any obstacle.

But everyone runs out of steam at some point, and there's a name for what happens then: the Peter Principle.

The continual change of jobs in pursuit of higher compensation works like a staircase. Someone steps up into a new position where they are ignorant and incompetent, and works hard to acquire knowledge and competence. Their reward is an opportunity to step up again and to repeat the cycle, until at last they reach a level of ignorance and incompetence that they are unable (or often unwilling) to overcome.

In the worst case, an old and established organization can be led completely by incompetent people, with all the work done by people further down the ladder.

While there are tools for leaders to combat this within an organization, it's important that you be self-aware and careful to avoid that one step too far up the staircase. Yes, you can move up, and you can make more, and you can overcome ignorance and incompetence over and over again. But take each step with your eyes open and with a commitment to moving ahead.

We each are willing to go only so far; it's good to know how far that is for you.

STEP 5

REACH FOR YOUR NEXT
MILESTONE

So far in this process you have identified your goal, started doing the next thing, set yourself up for success, and ensured you are in the right job to support your goal.

Now it's time to look ahead and keep moving forward. What is the next milestone on the way to the life you want? A promotion? Publishing a book? Your boss's job? Exhibiting your art?

Identify something concrete and specific, and then start.

Step One: Time

The first step in getting ahead is turning off your television. (And by television, I mean any video entertainment, online or over the air.)

You can't think when you are watching television. Television is a passive, lean-back experience. You don't get ahead by leaning back; you get ahead by leaning forward.

You don't get ahead by leaning back; you get ahead by leaning forward.

Television is a time trap. Whether it's broadcast television, where every commercial break teases the show that follows, or YouTube videos, where the end of one clip leads right to the next recommendation, the medium is focused on filling all your available time.

Is there useful, educational, and career-advancing material available on television? Of course. But it is a rare person who can focus on those few gems and resist being pushed deep into the couch cushions for hours on end. And every useful thing on television is available in a lean-forward format too. Read the book that inspired the movie.

A couple of hours of watching television to relax each evening is not a small indulgence. If you have a job and any family or social obligations, a couple of hours each evening are close to 100 percent of the time available in which to distinguish yourself from everyone else in similar circumstances. Your advancement depends on distinguishing yourself by doing, and if you compare your daily schedule to that of those around you, you'll find those couple of hours an evening to be a precious commodity.

If you really want to get ahead, give away your television and don't click the video links.

Television is the worst possible use of your time. Not only is it inferior to lean-forward learning and doing, it is inferior to spending time with other people.

The average American watches more than thirty hours a week of television. The likelihood of your getting the life you want is in inverse proportion to the time you spend watching television.

If you really want to get ahead, give away your television and don't click the video links.

HOURS OF TV PER WEEK	ADVANCEMENT PROSPECTS
30+	**YOU'LL BE FIRST LET GO IN A DOWNTURN.**
20-30	**YOU CAN PROBABLY HOLD THIS JOB FOR A LONG TIME, WITH FEW PROSPECTS FOR GROWTH.**
10-20	**WHEN THEY REALLY NEED SOMEONE, YOU'LL BE THE BEST CHOICE IN THE GROUP.**
1-10	**YOU ARE MAKING THINGS HAPPEN.**
0-1	**WATCH OUT WORLD!**

Step Two: Savings

Start saving money right now.

All the ambition and all the advice and all the inspiration in the world mean nothing if you're in desperate financial circumstances. The time it takes to learn and the doing that distinguishes are luxuries of someone with margin in their life. People who live paycheck to paycheck don't have much margin, and the slightest disruption in schedule or employment or financial need can start a downward spiral from which it is hard to escape, let alone advance.

If you only have two cents, put one of them aside.

Savings create margin. Savings give you time. Savings allow you to seize opportunities. Savings prevent you from being held hostage by a particular job or set of circumstances.

If you only have two cents, put one of them aside.

Step Three: Learning

This very moment you likely have on your person, or close at hand, a portal to all that is known of the world and humanity. The sum of human knowledge is available to you at no cost, and you can access it without moving from your chair.

Yes, this is just a dramatic way of describing the Internet. But the Internet is a pretty dramatic thing, and when it comes to learning, we haven't yet absorbed all the incredible implications. We live in a world where the conventional wisdom on education and educational institutions are all stuck in the past.

Today, learning isn't bound to books, classes, or instructors. Physical objects, specific class times, and geography are now irrelevant. You can learn anything, from how to tie a bowtie to how to bake a soufflé to nuclear physics, online.

This accessibility of information is unprecedented in human history, and it unlocks everyone's full potential: Education, the world's greatest investment, is now free. Heading back to school so you can get a better job was the go-to strategy of the pre-Internet generation. Today the Internet is every-school, and it's a lot cheaper. Going back to school is outrageously expensive.

Treat the Internet as the world's greatest library and classroom; eschew cat pictures.

Learn everything you can. Treat the Internet as the world's greatest library and classroom; eschew cat pictures.

Still, sometimes school is the only way. Occupational licensing or company policy or industry standards may require you to earn a diploma. You may need the structure of a classroom or thrive on personal instruction. In that case, take the initiative to maximize your investment.

Pick the right thing to study. We all know someone who headed off to college to study music / law / engineering / nursing only to switch majors or drop out a year later. They say, "It turns out I didn't like practicing all day / reading law / math / seeing blood."

Make sure you are pursuing the right education.

Don't be this person. Before you enroll, take the time to know if you'll be studying the right thing. Read a memoir of someone who worked in that area. Browse a textbook on the subject matter. Read online discussion boards where practitioners hang out. Sit in on a class, take an expert to coffee, or spend a day shadowing someone who works in that field.

The best way to maximize your investment in education is to make sure you are pursuing the right education!

Read ahead. When you get to school, you'll be given a map of your entire education plan. You'll see a list of every class you need to take. For each of these classes it is likely that a syllabus with the complete reading list and all the assignments is already online. Start reading.

Reading ahead maximizes the value of your classroom time. When you've read the textbook or assigned readings you'll be familiar with the vocabulary and the concepts. It will be easier to follow the instructor, easier to take notes, and you'll ask better, smarter questions. (Asking better questions not only gives you a better educational experience, but it also distinguishes you to the instructor as a better student—worthy of better grades and more attention.)

If there is any value to sitting in a classroom, as opposed to simply reading at home, that value is in the classroom, with the instructor and your classmates. The better prepared you are, the more value you can get from the people in the room—the real value of going to school—and the less time you'll waste on the basics you could acquire anywhere.

You will get more from formal education if you have prepared with informal education.

What is the next milestone you need to reach to achieve your goal? You don't need anyone's permission to start doing the next thing right now.

Do it as a volunteer. Find a nonprofit that could use help in the role you want next and offer your services as a volunteer.

Do it for a blog. Start a blog and put your work output there. If you can't create that output without actually having the job, describe or mock-up the output you would create.

JUST START NOW.

The act of doing, or even writing about doing, the next thing will teach you things you can't learn any other way. And that practice will help you choose the right next job while preparing you with the skills needed for that job. If you do it publicly on a blog, or even if you just write about the area, you may develop an audience that helps you grow or even helps you land or create that next opportunity.

Start now and you can show the world what you've already done.

Put your output in your portfolio; describe your activity on your résumé. Start now, and instead of waiting for the world to see your potential, you can show the world what you've already done.

How to Start

If you can just start doing the next milestone toward your goal, then do it.

If the milestone requires materials you don't have, consider doing it at a different scale with different materials.

If the milestone requires a position you don't have, write about what you would do if you had the position. Choose someone you can observe doing the thing you aspire to (either a public figure or a blogger or just someone you know) and observe their actions, then write about what you would do, or whether you agree or disagree with their choices.

If you can't do the milestone yet in any way, then write about it. Critique or analyze or simply report on what is happening in the space.

A theme can provide the structure you need to be consistent and develop skills. Consistent output in a specific area can help you develop an audience and open up new opportunities.

Here are a few examples of how you can start taking the next step if your goal is to get ahead in a particular job:

Architect. Start designing buildings. Draw them with a pencil, or model them in home design software. Build them from foam board or cardboard. Pick a theme and design buildings for different types of people, or imagine dwellings for different animals, or restaurants for different cuisines. If you aren't ready to create, then discuss: Choose a type of building, or the work of a specific architect, and create a series of articles discussing each project in turn.

Columnist. Don't wait to get the weekly column; just start writing it. Pick a theme and set a deadline. Hold yourself to the same standards for consistent length, format, and time of submission that you'd have if you were reporting to an editor.

Dental Hygienist. You may not be able to "start now" by putting your fingers in people's mouths, but you can start blogging about the field and interviewing local hygienists.

Publicist. Choose an imaginary client from fiction and appoint yourself their publicist. At the end of each chapter in the book write up a media and press relations plan. Contact a blogger and book yourself an interview, as your client, on their blog. Prove you can spin a villain's image or get great press for a forgotten hero of literature.

Presidential Speechwriter. Take a look at the president's calendar on the White House website and draft a speech for the next engagement.

Radio Host. Create a podcast and interview your friends and family. Narrate a summary of the morning's headlines and traffic first thing each morning. Set a standard length and learn the discipline of filling time and hitting cues.

Software Developer. Write an app or create a website. Pick a small problem (a tip calculator, a mortgage calculator, a childhood game) and take it from idea to finished application.

These are just ideas for inspiration. The key is to start now.

Take Your Boss's Job

Sometimes the next job you want is already filled by your boss. Start taking it over now.

Too many people are waiting for their boss to be promoted or to retire or to be hit by a bus. The little-understood truth is that one of the biggest things keeping your boss in their position is the question of who would do their job if they were promoted / retired / fired.

Be the answer.

Be the answer.

A good boss wants to see the people working for them succeed and knows that their own success is fueled by their team's growth. A good boss would love to have you take over parts of their job so they have time to be more productive, to grow, and to take over more of their boss's job. Even a lazy boss would love to have some of their workload taken away.

Take the initiative and identify something your boss does that you could take over. Depending on the task, either offer to take it over or simply do it. Say, "I know you're really busy. I'd be happy to prepare a draft of the budget for you to review; it would be a good learning exercise for me." Or, "I took the liberty of writing a design brief for the new product; it helped me understand our customers better. I'd appreciate your feedback, and feel free to steal anything useful from it."

You need to understand your boss and use the right approach for their personality, but there are some general guidelines that will help with good bosses.

Be specific. Don't waste time with a general "let me know if there's anything I can take off your plate" approach. Your boss is already assigning you tasks; this just adds extra pressure to think harder about what to assign you. Observe what your boss is doing, and then take the initiative to identify something you can do well on their behalf. Suggest (or perform) a specific task.

Don't create work. Taking part of someone's job should make their life easier, not harder. Avoid taking over tasks that might, if done wrong (or simply not as the boss desired), require cleanup as well as redoing. Present completed work as a draft contribution that can be accepted and edited or simply ignored. Make your request for feedback or review optional and without obligation.

Use learning as an excuse. Everybody is pro-learning; it looks bad to oppose it. Every boss is (or should be) in favor of their team learning new things. If you're going to presume to do some of your boss's job, it will come across as less threatening or arrogant if you describe it as a learning exercise.

Maybe your work is ten times better than your boss would do on this task; if so, let them see and acknowledge that and even take the credit for being such a great teacher / mentor / boss.

Don't worry about the credit. Let your boss build on your draft or incorporate your efforts into their work. A great boss will acknowledge and credit your contribution. Even if your extra effort isn't immediately visible, your boss will come to rely on you as a more useful contributor, and you'll be better positioned for the next step. Your networking, question-asking, and other efforts to get ahead will ensure that even a bad boss can't hide your growing value.

There are some bad bosses. There are bosses who will see your desire to take over some of their job as a threat to their own power or position. If your boss has already arrived at their level of incompetence and has nowhere to move up in the organization, they may not be interested in seeing you grow.

There are some bad bosses. Don't let this stop you.

Don't let this stop you. You either need to get out and move to a job where you have prospects for growth and advancement working for someone who wants to see you succeed, or you need to take your boss's job even more aggressively and make sure your ability to move up is visible higher in your organization.

This isn't about corporate politics or about moving people out of your way. It is every leader's responsibility to be growing leaders behind them, and when you run up against a leader who has given up on that responsibility, it is your obligation to move into a new position where your own growth can continue.

"Move up or move out" is a career management strategy in many large organizations, including the military. There's no reason you can't adopt it as your own personal plan.

Ambition is a treadmill.

You can get some healthy exercise that makes you stronger, or you can spend lots of time wearing yourself out for diminishing returns.

You need to decide what is right for you. There isn't a right or wrong goal. There is no embarrassment in a market wage for a job you enjoy, and there is nothing wrong with skipping the employment path completely. The life you've always wanted may involve climbing a ladder, or it may be following a passion down a never-explored path.

Own your responsibility for yourself.

Own your freedom to choose the work and compensation and circumstances you want.

Own your action plan for getting ahead.

If you learn to be intentional, then you can choose to be content where you are or to set your sights on a new goal. Intentionality can help free you from doubt, from envy, and from self-reproach.

YOU CAN START NOW.

Start Now: Share Your Story

What is the life you've always wanted?
What are you going to do to create it? Email me at
bob@startnextnow.com and tell me about it! I want
to hear how you are going to start your next now.

THERE IS

MORE

ONLINE!

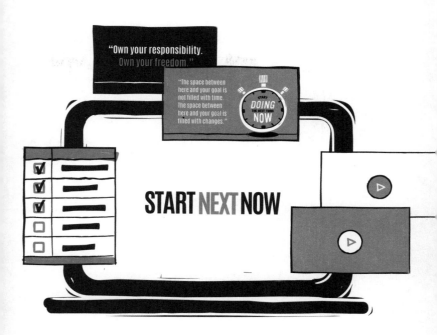

**VISIT STARTNEXTNOW.COM
FOR AN INTERACTIVE READING
EXPERIENCE, INTERVIEWS, AND
MORE IDEAS ON HOW YOU CAN
START NEXT NOW!**

Acknowledgements

I feel blessed beyond measure to have the life I've always wanted: working with talented people, creating awesome products, constantly learning, and sharing the whole experience with family and friends. This book, which started as conversations with employees about making more money and achieving goals, is a byproduct of that experience.

My parents, Dale and Jenni Pritchett, gave me the permission to try anything and all the support and encouragement a child could need. I owe them everything.

My wife, Audra, is my first and most important sounding board, a constant encouragement, and an invaluable critic of my writing. Our children, Jacob and Kaiti, both read early drafts and shared feedback from their unique perspectives.

Anne-Marie Faiola, Jim Straatman, and Bradley Grainger provided early feedback on the theme of the book. Breanna Bart, Ray Deck, Justin Marr, Brannon Ellis, Franklin Goldberg, Phil Gons, Chris duMond, and Eli Evans all provided useful feedback and contributions, and dozens of team members at Faithlife participated in discussions, focus groups, and reviewing drafts.

It was a pleasure to work with Jennifer Stair as an editor; she greatly improved the writing and found the organizing theme for the book. What remains weak reflects only my stubbornness.

Josh Warren did a fantastic job with the cover and illustrations, and Brittany VanErem pulled it all together with creative typesetting and layout.

About the Author

Bob Pritchett started a business at age 19 and leads it today. In 24 years Faithlife Corporation (formerly Logos Bible Software) has grown to more than 440 employees serving more than 3 million users around the world. Over years of mentoring interns, promoting employees, and raising two kids, Bob has learned exactly what life and career advice young people need most, and how rare it is for any of them to take it. But what amazing stuff happens when they do!

Bob is a 2005 winner of the Ernst & Young Entrepreneur of the Year award, one of Glassdoor's Hightest Rated CEOs 2015, and was included in the Puget Sound Business Journal's 40 Under 40. (Several years ago.) He blogs at BobPritchett.com.

Bob's first book, *Fire Someone Today, And Other Surprising Tactics for Making Your Business a Success*, was published in 2006 and has been translated into Russian and Korean.

"Bob's book is like a year's worth of lunches with someone who has been way down the road and taken a lot of lumps—who can now help you avoid repeating his mistakes. And you only have to buy once."—GUY KAWASAKI

FireSomeoneToday.com